50 Ways
To Attract
And
Keep Clients

Sonya Gill

ISBN:1973924722
ISBN-13: 978-1973924722

DEDICATION

I dedicate this book to everyone who has participated as a teacher in my life.

GET TO KNOW ME

I've been in the field of marketing for the past 13 years, and to be honest, it was completely by default.

From as far back as I can remember, I think I always had a mic in my hand. At the age of 4 I would pretend to interview invisible people, attempting to record my first solo album at the age of 8 (I can't sing worth crap), speaking about what motivates people at the age of 12, to writing contests and speeches at assemblies all throughout high school. Communications has always been my thing.

But what really catapulted my career is when I dropped out of University at the age of 22 with a minor in communications, a one way ticket to Toronto and a vision the size of Mount Everest. It was about 3 months into my move to Toronto when I realized the courses I was taking at a local college (pre-communications for Journalism) were not what I needed. What I needed was to get on the streets and learn the hard way….through internships and failing fast. And that is just what I did. I learned about communications in quite possibly every form known to man. From video editing, public speaking, photography and branding, there was no rock I left unturned. And this was all before the age of social media.

Fast forward to present day and I can proudly say I survived an 8 year career in television and radio, but can also say that those 8 years also taught me a lot in communications and branding. To date I have taught close to 150 social media workshops across Canada and spoken at numerous Entrepreneurship seminars. I built a digital marketing agency which was acquired in 2015 and am presently running a company under my moniker at SG Communications where I assist to provide results for small businesses and Fortune 500 companies.

And to be honest, although a lot of my knowledge in marketing comes from taking classes, majority of my knowledge comes from reading books. So I wanted to write this book to share some of my favourite quotes from some of the most admired authors and walk you through what those quotes meant to me and regurgitate what I took away from them. In turn, my wish is that you are able to walk away from this book inspired and filled with new ideas to take back to your business, team and clients. Of if anything, just a simple 'a ha' moment.

Hope you enjoy this book as much as I enjoyed creating it!

LET'S BEGIN.

"IN A CROWDED MARKETPLACE, FITTING IN IS A FAILURE. IN A BUSY MARKETPLACE, NOT STANDING OUT IS THE SAME AS BEING INVISIBLE." - SETH GODIN

One of the things that Seth Godin advises is if you have to copy, don't copy from your competitor; copy from someone who's from a different industry instead. This will help you stand out in your industry.

There have been many times when I've had people come to me and say, "I really like how this person markets their brand" OR there are other times when I've helped someone build their website and they have sent me 5 examples of sites they really like from their industry. See the common theme?

Numerous ideas are recycled, but the best ideas are when they are reinvented with a different pair of glasses. Never forget that you only have one opportunity to make a first impression, and the best first impression is one that is refreshing.

"IT'S IMPORTANT TO BUILD A PERSONAL BRAND BECAUSE IT'S THE ONLY THING YOU'RE GOING TO HAVE, ESPECIALLY IN THE NEW AGE OF BUSINESS. YOUR REPUTATION ONLINE IS THE NEW GAME. SO BE A NICE PERSON AND GET OUT THERE ON SOME LEVEL - GARY VAYNERCHUK

I cannot stress this enough. However, you also don't want to build a brand you have absolutely no passion about, because then you risk getting type casted and one day in the future when you want to change gears in your career, you will always be known as the person who did 'that'.

But as Gary Vaynerchuk says, it's definitely important to build your personal brand. And in my professional opinion, good brand building comes with storytelling and if you have a personal story to tell through your brand, you're right on track. If you achieve this, this is where you will begin to see opportunities appear.

Remember though, never lose your integrity while building your brand. Stay true to your values and beliefs and people will keep coming back.

"HIGH CREATIVITY IS RESPONDING TO SITUATIONS
WITHOUT CRITICAL THOUGHT" - PAUL ARDEN

Have you ever come up with a great idea only to Google it and find out it already exists? And then your idea goes to complete shit? As I've said before, ideas are recycled and borrowed and the more you pollute your original idea with too much thought, ideations, and opinions, the creativity that surrounded your initial thought process has been squashed.

And don't be afraid of silly ideas, look at the wine Fat Bastard as an example. Could you imagine being in a wine store and you see all these fancy bottles with names that are so hard to pronounce it makes your head hurt? And then all of a sudden you see Fat Bastard? The marketing is simply ingenious. And actually, thinking about silly ideas helps you overcome mental blocks because sometimes we are so hard on ourselves trying to come up with a perfect solution, we are stopping ourselves from being creative.

So do yourself a favour next time you come up with an idea. Just run with it, don't over research it, and definitely bring out the kid in you to help you bring it to life.

"BOIL THE FROG" - UNKNOWN

There's an old wives' tale that if you put a frog in boiling water, it will sense the heat and jump out. But put a frog in cool water and turn up the heat slowly and the frog will hardly notice.

When reaching out online to people you'd like to meet, don't come on like gangbusters. Nothing screams "jump out of the hot pot" more than a blatant "let's talk so I can sell you something" message.

Start cool and warm up slowly. Comment on their blog post. Retweet them thoughtfully. Compliment something they wrote. Become familiar to someone—even if they don't engage you right away—and it's more likely that they'll engage you in the future.

Dr. Rachna Jain, who studies the psychology of social media, says, "When people see you more, they like you more. The shorthand is that familiarity breeds likeability. Especially if you're seen as giving them value or good content or information."

"IF YOUR STORIES ARE ALL ABOUT YOUR PRODUCTS AND SERVICES, THAT'S NOT STORYTELLING. IT'S A BROCHURE. GIVE YOURSELF PERMISSION TO MAKE THE STORY BIGGER." - JAY BAER

Sometimes we get carried away when we get online and begin marketing our businesses. We want the world to know what we do and feel the burning desire to share all the products and services we can provide. But what happens more often than not is we become so confined by the walls in our minds of how we 'should' advertise that we forget that the story behind the product also exists and that it is ultimately up to us to showcase that story and make it bigger. It's up to you to connect that story to your business and share it with your market. They deserve to know more about you as a person as well as your business and it's customers.

So stop selling and telling, instead share your story and invite people into your life. Think of it like throwing a housewarming party and inviting 50 friends. You wouldn't just start handing them brochures would you?

"SOCIAL MEDIA CREATES COMMUNITIES, NOT MARKETS." - DON SCHULTZ

First things first, market like you mean it. Authentically say things that you can back up and don't say things for the sake of saying them. This is also called personal branding.

However, the moment you start any type of engagement on social media, you must not allow yourself to stop. Remember, you are not creating a market, you are about to create a community.

Challenge yourself to think about what your intentions are and what you are capable of delivering to the communities and people you are serving. If you are able to do this with honesty and integrity, you will absolutely create a community.

Every day you must deliver a standard of expectation that you have set forth for not only your company but yourself. You don't want to look like spam, and you don't want to look like you are boasting. Try to find a happy medium. Put yourself in your audience's shoes.

"CONTENT BUILDS RELATIONSHIPS, RELATIONSHIPS ARE BUILT ON TRUST, TRUST DRIVES REVENUE." - ANDREW DAVIS

Today almost all consumers are using the world wide web to search for solutions to their queries. They read up on customer reviews on Yelp and in turn will research products and product reviews. They ultimately base their purchasing decisions on the information they find online.

Your future customers need to know more about your company and it's products if they are about to embark on a business relationship with you. Why? Because they want to feel that they have a unique and personal relationship with their favourite brand, product and/or service. Once a customer feels they can trust you, of course they are going to do business with you.

Therefore, you need to ensure that you are executing content at the highest caliber. Ensure that you are relaying information that is honest and can create a positive or memorable impact. Ensure that you have a team of highly creative community members that can assist with telling your story online.

"PEOPLE ARE IN SUCH A HURRY TO LAUNCH THEIR PRODUCT OR BUSINESS THAT THEY SELDOM LOOK AT MARKETING FROM A BIRD'S EYE VIEW AND THEY DON'T CREATE A SYSTEMATIC PLAN". - DAVE RAMSEY

I would be lying if I said I did this in the beginning when launching my first business. I mean, I knew what I was doing, but I didn't really KNOW what I was doing. And most entrepreneurs actually start off like this because they don't have a marketing department, they are the marketing department.

It's understandable that with the big picture in mind (after all that's what us entrepreneurs are known for), all the minuscule stuff becomes overwhelming and most of us don't even know where to begin. But my advice to those starting out is start from the top and work your way down. So for example, if your goal is 100 clients a month, work your way down until you have broken down your marketing strategy into numerical steps.

In order to be phenomenal at marketing you must be focused. You need to look at the demand in the marketplace, the scarcity and activity of your future clients and/or users. Then you can proceed from there.

"REMEMBER THAT THE 6 MOST EXPENSIVE WORDS IN BUSINESS IS: WE'VE ALWAYS DONE IT THAT WAY". - CATHERINE DEVRYE

When was the last time you were in a boardroom with a potential client and you tried to pitch them a new idea and they shot it down? This not only happens more often than not in boardrooms, but also in fortune 500 companies where the ladder to the final decision maker just doesn't end. People are afraid of changing their ways, because why fix something if it isn't broken, right?

I have one rule of thumb in building my brand and with those that I coach. Keep moving, your competition is right behind you. You MUST keep innovating, keep executing and keep on your toes because chances are someone will surpass you if you continue doing things the way you've always done them.

Past success is no guarantee of future success. You must be quality and customer focused, so much so that you understand when to change directions at a drop of a dime. Otherwise your customers may find someone else that can.

"A BUSINESS HAS ONLY TWO FUNCTIONS: MARKETING AND INNOVATION". - PETER DRUCKER

Marketing attracts clients and innovation is how you will continuously deliver to your clients. Everything else you do in your business supports these two main components.

Gone are the days when companies had less competition. In today's world of social media and the rate at which technology changes everyday, companies need to be quicker on their feet to respond to problems, customer feedback and most importantly their competitors.

However, if you say, "but Sonya, our product is different, there's nothing else like it on the market", I'd say, that is great, but better products don't always win. It's how you market these products and the perception of those watching your products that matters the most. Every aspect of your communication needs to reflect your difference - this is if you are telling me you are innovative enough.

From your advertising, your marketing materials, your website, sales presentation, and online presence. Your innovation and marketing must fit like a hand in glove.

"TAKE TWO IDEAS AND PUT THEM TOGETHER TO MAKE ONE NEW IDEA. AFTER ALL, WHAT IS A SNUGGIE BUT THE MUTATION OF A BLANKET AND A ROBE?" - JIM KUKRAL

Competition in a particular industry happens when too many brands try to copy each other. This leads to saturation and nothing innovative can come from this.

However, if you look outside of your industry for inspiration there's probably a good chance that you can take two ideas and put them together to make one great new idea.

Some people say that it's hard to come up with new ideas and that they are not creative. This is a misperception. If you are always on the lookout for new ideas and travel outside of your comfort zone, your chances of coming up with a new strategy or new product are very high.

And remember, more often than not we let our biases creep in and judge our thinking. What you need to do is forget everything you know and begin looking at everything from a fresh perspective. Leave all of your preconceived ideas and opinions in the past. They are of no use when it comes to thinking of new ideas!

"IF YOU WANT TO GO FAST, GO ALONE. IF YOU WANT TO GO FAR, GO WITH OTHERS." - AFRICAN PROVERB

Why is it when we get cold emails from people, our first reaction is to hit delete or completely ignore their existence?

Networking is only ever successful when it happens in real life. And the only way it can happen is if you allow it to. Think of the last person who asked if they could just get 5 minutes of your time? The first thing you probably did was ignore them, right? Think about if you actually did go out to coffee with this person who was trying to sell you empty toilet paper rolls. Who cares what they are trying to sell you! Do you know the endless possibilities of who this person could be related to or connected with?

I understand that cold emails are annoying and I would be lying if I said I was also not guilty of ignoring these emails. But what if you actually replied with a YES? What if today we decide collectively we are going to say YES to every person who tries to sell us empty toilet rolls from here on?

"IT IS WRONG TO BE RIGHT". - PAUL ARDEN

Being right is based upon knowledge and experience and is often provable.

Knowledge comes from the past, so it's safe. It is also out of date. It's the opposite of originality. Experience is built from solutions to old situations and problems. The old situations are probably different from the present ones, so that old solutions will have to be bent to fit new problems. Also the likelihood is that, if you've got the experience, you'll probably use it. This is lazy. Experience is the opposite of being creative. If you can prove you're right you're set in concrete. You cannot move with the times or with other people. Being right is also being boring. Your mind is closed. You are not open to new ideas. You are rooted in your own rightness, which is arrogant. Arrogance is a valuable tool, but only if used very sparingly. Worst of all, being right has a tone of morality about it. To be anything else sounds weak or fallible, and people who are right would hate to be thought fallible.

So: it's wrong to be right, because people who are right are rooted in the past, rigid-minded, dull and smug. There's no talking to them.

Be original in your marketing. Stop following experience.

"DON'T BE AFRAID TO GET CREATIVE AND EXPERIMENT WITH YOUR MARKETING." - MIKE VOLPE

There are a lot of brands out there that quit their marketing game too early because it's just not working for them. They either don't want to continue spending more money, of just like a person on a diet, quit too soon before seeing any results.

The thing with marketing, especially online, is you need to constantly re-evaluate your goals, your strategy and perhaps pull the plug on one of your social networks or endeavours that is just not working for you anymore. Sometimes brands, as marketers, end up on the wrong social platforms and end up using the wrong tools which is why they are not getting the answers they need to adjust their strategy. Remember that what works for one business, might not work for yours.

Sometimes you need to delve deep and look at the quality of your content. It's not enough to keep feeding your clients the same content, nor is it fair. Social media is social for a reason. Focus on improving the quality of your content, the consistency and most importantly create content that is designed for humans to interact with, not just to get leads. Be the brand that people genuinely want to follow and read content from every day.

"FOCUS ON THE CORE PROBLEM YOUR BUSINESS SOLVES AND PUT OUT LOTS OF CONTENT AND ENTHUSIASM AND IDEAS ABOUT HOW TO SOLVE THAT PROBLEM." – LAURA FITTON

If you follow me on social media, you know that I enjoy putting out information. A lot of information. I do this because I want my followers to know that a) I understand what I am talking about b) I'm trying to assist businesses with their aches and pains and c) I know that honest communication breeds authentic relationships.

The best way to show people that you know what you are talking about is to give away information for free. I chuckle when someone says to me, "but you should get paid for all the material you are putting out there!" This is untrue. Because if someone is good at assisting people on a surface level, imagine how good they would be at solving problems if you actually worked with them one-on-one?

Sometimes focusing on your company's online presence is a necessity. It not only enhances your brand, but speaks for your product and/or service. If you are able to deliver examples, information, and proof of what you do, imagine how impressed your customers will be when they actually begin working with you. Remember, customers breed customers.

"JUST BECAUSE YOU CAN MEASURE EVERYTHING DOESN'T MEAN THAT YOU SHOULD." – W. EDWARD DEMING

You should always start with the question, 'what am I going to do with all of this data?' Because if you don't have a strategy and just wanted to know the results, then you are just looking at a bunch of numbers. And looking at numbers without understanding the context behind it will give you funny results.

Let's take Hurricane Sandy for example, one would be a fool to correlate the volume of tweets to the degree of destruction (there were less tweets during the hurricane as communication towers were knocked out and cell phone batteries had died) or say if you measure your company's online success by the number of likes and followers it receives. This would be ridiculous.

There are also times where you may push out a massive online ad campaign only to have the results come back sub par. But instead of thinking 'we got poor results, so we should stop our marketing', why not think instead that perhaps your endeavours were too pushy and driving consumers away?

"IF YOU WAIT UNTIL THERE IS ANOTHER CASE STUDY IN YOUR INDUSTRY, YOU WILL BE TOO LATE." - SETH GODIN

There is also another famous quote by the founder of LinkedIn, Reid Hoffman, that if you have reached perfection by the time you have launched, it's probably too late. Both Seth Godin and Reid have very valuable points and to be honest as a perfectionist myself, I usually look before I leap where I should actually be jumping.

When we market our brand or wait to execute a product, most of us wait too long. What if we receive backlash? What if no one likes it? What if we turn customers away? All of these questions haunt us, but the truth is is how will you ever know unless you have tried (god, I really need to take my own advice sometimes). You could read a hundred case studies of successful and not so successful companies, but you won't truly know the answer until you execute. And in this case, you are actually conducting your own case study by doing so.

Case studies, again, only give us surface level information, it's hard to know the context in most of these studies unless you were actually physically there yourself.

"CLARITY TRUMPS PERSUASION."
- DR. FLINT MCGLAUGHLIN

Many brands are intimidated by choosing the best messaging, the best branding, the best influencer. But one of the most important ways to attract clients and/or users is to write like you speak. Forget all the fluff, forget the pretty corporate wording, just stick to plain english. Write like you were to speak to your customers.

Research has found that the most traffic and gain occurs in the first seven seconds of a user's experience. Millions of dollars, if not millions of downloads, are won or lost in these first few moments a visitor spends on your site and if they are unable to figure out what you are trying to sell them, then you've lost your customer.

Most people are led to your site or product because they wanted to go there. But if once they are there and there is no clarity on the product, and they cannot understand what they are purchasing and they are unable to find the information they are looking for, well guess what, they aren't buying from you.

Ultimately, the deciding factor of a purchase is not how persuasive you or your copy was, but rather how much of it they understood. I always say, if you can't explain it to your 5 year old niece, then you don't understand it.

"GOOGLE ONLY LOVES YOU WHEN EVERYONE LOVES YOU FIRST" - WENDY PIERSALL

When you tell someone you can get them on the first page of Google, their eyes light up and you can see dollar signs in their eyes. But when you tell them it's going to take at least 3 months to begin the process, they lose their enthusiasm. It's the truth though, that is the minimum amount of time it will take you for you to get your brand on the first page of Google. There is no magic algorithm (they nixed the illegal way of doing it years ago), but there is a ton of content marketing that goes into it.

Let's look at your website like a high school popularity contest. The more people that know about you, the more noise and buzz you create, the more credibility you get. And in turn, Google recognizes this and begins to follow you, because they want in on the piece of action, which in result gives you a better ranking. And imagine if you are consistent in your actions, over a period of 3 months, you'll be the talk around town.

This is why it is important to have a content marketer. These individuals can assist you with every aspect of online marketing. A position you shouldn't just leave up to anyone. This person is your ticket onto the first page of Google.

"BRANDS NEED TO BUILD DIGITAL RELATIONSHIPS BEFORE CLOSING A SALE." - CHRIS BROGAN

Does your company have a brand loyalty program or do you just take email addresses for the sake of taking them? Do you send your customers stuff they can brag about and benefit from?

What types of relationships you develop with your clients online matters. It matters because you never know when a client will become a whistleblower, this is when a client will rant and rave about a product or company because they just can't get enough and they would like to personally see the company succeed. These are not only whistleblowers, but they are brand advocates. And the more brand advocates you can build, the better your brand reputation.

These types of relationships are developed when you take care of your clients. When you see your client was having a bad day, or just got engaged, or just announced they are having a baby. These are your chances to pay attention and go the extra mile for your customers. This is where key relationships are formed and customers become those for life.

"YOU PROBABLY HAVE A DEVICE THAT CAN SHOOT DECENT VIDEO, SO WHAT'S STOPPING YOU?" - STEVE GARFIELD

There's SnapChat, Instagram Story and as of recently Facebook Live. And if you are not using any one of these to market your brand, you are behind. As the quote says, you most likely have a camera (on your phone), so what is stopping you?

When I consult my clients, one of the top suggestions I give them is branding through the conduit that is video. People are nosey and they want to see what you are doing, they want to see behind the scenes footage, what you eat for breakfast, who you hang out with, what your husband or wife looks like. They want to know all of this stuff, because once they see some of those parts, they begin to feel as though they know you.

However, there may be times that you are just too much of a perfectionist and don't want to put out certain footage because you just wished it looked better. But guess what, with a flood of apps on the market that are used by thousands of people, you too can make your video look great by using one of them (Google is your best friend on this). And actually, one of the best short movies to have ever come to Sundance was shot with an iPhone 5S!

"EVEN WHEN YOU ARE MARKETING TO YOUR ENTIRE AUDIENCE OR CUSTOMER BASE, YOU ARE STILL SIMPLY SPEAKING TO A SINGLE HUMAN AT ANY GIVEN TIME."
– ANN HANDLEY

Have you ever scrolled through your social media feed and stopped on a particular post because you felt it spoke to you? And then you went to check out the individual's profile to see who they were? Think about this every single time you post something. You may not get a thousand views or likes, but the mere fact that you may have affected 2-3 people is more beneficial to you.

Why?

Because when you consistently affect individuals instead of a plethora of people, your chances of building a tribe of advocates is much higher. Remember the term whistleblowers from the previous page? You want to make it your goal to build more of these kinds of cheerleaders.

There is a lot of sameness in our world, and you need to remember that in a given day people are feeling either bad, good or great. That, and we also live in world where things are going on ALL the time, it's not that hard to come up with a clever post. So to affect those 2-3 people in your feed is actually not as hard as you think it may be.

"GOOD MARKETING MAKES THE COMPANY LOOK SMART.
GREAT MARKETING MAKES THE CUSTOMER FEEL SMART."
– JOE CHERNOV

When was the last time you delved so deep into analytics that you could answer every one of the following questions:

<u>WHO</u> DEMOGRAPHICS
<u>WHAT</u> THEY USE
<u>WHAT</u> THEY CONSUME
<u>WHAT</u> THEY DO
<u>WHAT</u> THEY BUY
<u>WHERE</u> THEY USE
<u>WHERE</u> THEY BUY
<u>WHERE</u> THEY CONSUME
<u>WHERE</u> THEY SEE
<u>WHY</u> VALUES
<u>WHY</u> EMOTIONS

The thing is, you need to understand that real people exist behind your data. And the more you know about your customers, the better you can suit their needs.

A customer needs to feel that they are making a smart choice by buying your product. They also need to feel proud so when they brag to their friends you feel proud of YOU and the legacy you have built.

"THE KEY TO CREATIVITY AND INNOVATION IS EMPATHY"
– BRIAN SOLIS

Sometimes as business owners we spend so much time pondering the best way to reach our audience that we forget that just like us, they are viewers too. It truly requires a degree of empathy to figure out what your audience is going to respond to.

Empathy is the ability to intellectually and emotionally connect with an experience, it's one of humanity's defining characteristics. And if there is anything we can learn from research it is that we don't see anything or anyone the way they are, we see them as we want to and because of this we often end up putting out content or products that most people don't resonate with. So what is the trick?

I always tell my clients that you must look at your own behaviours and understand why you click or share something. If you can understand what makes your thumbs move on your phone or makes you hoot and holler about a certain ad, post or video, you will soon begin to understand the emotional side of human nature. Ultimately your goal should be to put out something that is going to make people a) laugh b) cry c) think d) motivate or e) get them fired up.

"WRITE GREAT HEADLINES AND YOU'LL HAVE
SUCCESSFULLY INVESTED 80% OF YOUR MONEY."
- DAVID OGILVY

Less is more when it comes to titles. Did you know that 8 out of 10 people only read the headline? That leaves just 2 out of 10 who stay and read the rest of the article. With these numbers, do you really think people can afford to waste their time reading something complicated or tricky, that makes them think even more? People need just the right amount of information, that in only a few seconds seduces them to linger a little longer.

Basically with a great advertising headline, what we need the reader to tell us: "Ok, you got my attention, now, tell me more."

When David Ogilvy took on Rolls-Royce as a customer, he spent three weeks reading and studying all the technical characteristics of the car until he came up with the phrase "60 miles per hour, the loudest noise comes from the electric clock". That became the title, and the rest of the sales pamphlet was composed of 607 words of copy.

People also do this with Facebook articles every day! Only the ones with the catchiest titles ever get clicked on and read.

"DO IT FOR THE GHOST FOLLOWERS" - ME!

By ghost followers, I don't mean fake accounts. I mean people who creep you online. And remember, analytics don't lie.

For example, as I write this I have 2300 followers on Instagram, but my analytics constantly tell me that my posts are seen about 25-30k times and I have about 8,000 unique profile views (these are people that don't necessarily follow me).

You can't get stuck on the number of people following you and think that it's not worth building your brand because you don't have enough followers. Rome wasn't built in a day and neither will your brand be.

Keep building your online brand because remember, people ARE looking at your stuff. Think of it like a good YouTube Channel, we may not necessarily follow the person online, but we will talk about it with friends and family if we think it's good. And guess what, that's where the real buzz begins to happen.

"SWAP AUTO RESPONSES FOR GENUINE INTERACTIONS" - TIM FERRISS

Do you find yourself copying and pasting your msgs via LinkedIn or email when looking for clients or trying to connect with someone?

Energy can be read very easily and what you say in your emails has a huge impact on how your relationship is going to play out with the receiving party.

One of the best tricks I've learned that has worked over the years is a simple one liner asking a question. So say for example I want to reach out to someone whom I don't know, but I know that a) they have a blog and b) they own a business. I would start the email by putting into the subject heading 'Blog', and in the body of the email I would say, "Hi (insert name here), My name is Sonya Gill and I had a few questions about your blog regarding (X). If and when you have a moment, could you let me know when would be a good time to chat?

Not only is this email short and to the point, but notice I am not asking anything for myself and I have made it about the other person? It's short enough to pique curiosity and genuine so the person is likely to reply. Try it!

"EXCLUSIVITY AND HIGH PRICES DON'T SIGNIFY PRESTIGE ANYMORE, AS TECHNOLOGY HAS LEVELLED THE PLAYING FIELD". - WOLFGANG SCHAEFER

A strategy that doesn't work as well as it once did is high pricing. Brands were once able to distinguish themselves through luxurious price tags and the idea was that a product would become a status symbol when only a select few movers and shakers could afford it.

However, now anyone can buy or borrow the prestige of a brand. Online sales offer designer clothes at a discount while luxury cars can be rented by the hour. As a result, some luxury items have lost their lacklustre.

The new status driver is now knowledge. This means that your brand can attain prestige by being in the know. A knowledgeable brand can actually help customers appear knowledgeable as privileged information is sometimes necessary to 'get' a brand. A good example is a skater who distinguishes herself from posers by only wearing 'real' skater gear.

Another aspect of establishing brand prestige today is the need to be honest and ethical in your business dealings. As we see everyday, information about a company's unethical behaviour can destroy a luxury brand.

"GROWTH HACKING IS A NEW, LOW-BUDGET FORM OF MARKETING AIMED AT RAPID GROWTH" - RYAN HOLIDAY

Today's top companies like Dropbox and Groupon, are now household names, but there are a few tricks behind how they built their name.

Instead of taking the traditional approach to marketing and buying huge billboards and newspaper ads, these companies used growth hacker marketing. Whereas traditional marketers ask, 'How can I get customers', these growth hackers used technology to answer that question by tracking user behaviour and adjusting their strategy accordingly.

Remember when Dropbox would offer free space for simply telling friends about their app and viewing their tutorial video? That is an example of low-budget marketing while getting the word out at the same time.

And the thing with these companies is because they didn't have large marketing budgets to start with, growth hacking allowed them to optimize their product over time by simply studying the analytics of their customers.

CREATIVE PEOPLE ARE SHAPING SOCIETY AND COMPANIES SHOULD ATTEND TO THEIR NEEDS. - PHILIP KOTLER

New forms of advertising are emerging and creating a new economy in which an increasing number of people work in the creative sector as filmmakers, writers, website designers and so on.

While these creative workers still represent a relatively small sector of society, they exert a significant influence as they have sophisticated desires that demand a new approach to business and marketing. This new set of creative individuals don't just lust after material possessions. For them, making the world better while finding meaning, happiness and spirituality are stronger drives than the lust for material possessions.

If you can, you should carefully curate your message through your marketing campaigns with this new economy in mind and follow through with that same messaging in your actions. This will go a far way amongst this new crowd that is likely to tell others.

"SUCCESS LEAVES CLUES, BUT IT WON'T MAKE YOU REMARKABLE". - SETH GODIN

Another popular, but poor, strategy for businesses is "follow the leader" and a lot of motivational 'success gurus' also encourage others to follow this mantra. However, it is not the greatest advice one could give.

Basically, if you 'follow the leader', you are mimicking the actions of the leaders in their field. But if you use this strategy, it will never actually make you a leader yourself. And we see this happen with brands on Instagram all the time.

This is because the leaders likely attained their success by taking risks and creating something exceptional. If you just imitate others, do you think you will ever become remarkable?

Being in a competitive marketplace is a good thing. It should actually encourage you to become more innovative, not to succumb to what the 'cool' kids are doing and just copy. Force yourself to think outside of the box!

"WE ARE MOST INFLUENCED BY PRODUCTS, IDEAS AND
BEHAVIOURS IF WE OBSERVE THEM FREQUENTLY."
- JONAH BERGER

If a behaviour (or product, or idea) is observable, its influence and contagiousness is increased. That's because we tend to imitate the behaviours of others. Let's take for example the men's health awareness campaign "Movember," which encourages men to grow mustaches during the month of November. As men witnessed others taking part in the campaign, their curiosity was piqued and they joined in. In this case, the effect of such contagious behaviour was that it raised awareness of men's health issues.

So why do we imitate the behaviour of those around us? One explanation is social proof: we do what others are doing because we assume that since it appears to be so popular, there has to be a good reason for doing it. Take the ALS Ice Bucket Challenge as another example.

Thus, the next time you decide to launch a marketing campaign or set to brand yourself or a product online, look into the emotions that the campaign can actually carry. Studies have actually shown that campaigns or articles written to provoke emotion are the most likely to go viral.

"TO IMAGINE WHAT PROGRESS THE FUTURE WILL BRING, YOU MUST BE ABLE TO VIEW THE PRESENT DIFFERENTLY."
- PETER THIEL

A person who can think outside established conventions has the ability to see the future. Now just imagine if you were able to deliver outstanding, creative, never have thought before products and services to your clients time and time again? Apple comes to mind doesn't it?

Thus, you have to learn to become the architect of your own future and make a focused effort to attain it. You've got to do things differently than you did them before. You need to have a laser fuelled focus on perfecting your service and have an understanding of how to deliver it 10 different ways. Because you're just that good at it.

Success is the product of focus, dedication and determination. Fate and luck have little to do with it. Businesses only have one best future, and attaining it demands a concerted effort. Day in and day out. No questions asked. How do you think Steve Jobs or Peter Thiel founded several prosperous businesses and thousands of dedicated customers?

"IF YOU WANT TO BE INTERESTING, BE INTERESTED IN OTHERS" - DALE CARNEGIE

We all love a good listener, especially when that person encourages us to speak about ourselves. Now imagine if you did that with every customer in your business? Humans are always happy to meet people who are interested in them.

Imagine you went out of way to shake hands with 10 of your top customers. You got to know their name, their great aunt's name and hey, maybe even the name of their favourite cheese. Do you know how much they would adore you? They would adore you because you took the time out of your schedule to listen to them. You encouraged them to speak about themselves and you actually cared to know more about them. And in turn you have probably turned this customer into a loyal friend for life.

Take the time to Google people, find them on Facebook and LinkedIn. Try to find out as much detail you can about them, as if you were preparing for a job interview and watch the likability take form. Now you may say, Sonya that's unattainable because I have over 500 clients. But remember, I said pick 10. You can do that right?

"ONCE A CLIENT CANCELS A SERVICE, THAT DOESN'T MEAN YOU SAY SAYONARA!" - JILL GRIFFIN

When a customer cancels your service, or wants to cancel your service, there's a big opportunity for you to not only prevent them from leaving but also to improve the reputation of your business, save money and win more customers.

If you think about it, just the loss of a single long-term customer means that your company has to expend resources, marketing materials, sales and personnel costs just to acquire a new customer. You have to remember there is a reason that customers leave in the first place and you need to uncover this WHY. Not only can it save you hundreds of dollars, but it would be a huge learning lesson of what not to do down the road.

Imagine you run a yoga studio and have lost a customer. Because there are only a small number of people who live in your neighbourhood and practice yoga, losing that one customer is a pretty big deal. You just don't know when your next customer is going to walk through the door. Similarly, this one customer is just as big of a deal for the rival yoga studio down the street. Learn to create a win back program to gain these kinds of clients back.

"INFLUENCE PEOPLE WITH STORYTELLING,
MOTIVATIONAL TECHNIQUES AND DIRECT EXPERIENCES."
- JOSEPH GRENNY

If you want to influence people's behaviour, you need to convince them of your way of thinking. One way to do this is through motivational content and the other is storytelling. I always say to my clients, when you begin to brand yourself online, you must come with a story. You need to walk people through your journey or the journey of your brand.

Think of a good book. There's a beginning, middle and end. And usually our interest is piqued somewhere towards the middle when the story gets really good. This is exactly what you need to get through to your clients and get them hooked. This is also how you build a tribe of loyal followers.

The way you present your products or services also directly impacts your influence over your customers because beautiful things make us curious. And if we are able to touch them and try them out we have been silently influenced by you.

"USE A MENTAL TRIGGER IN THE MARKETING OF YOUR IDEA" - JEFF WALKER

Mental triggers are suppose to exploit the part of the brains programming to direct us toward making particular decisions over others. And to function efficiently, the brain tends to take shortcuts when making a judgement. Subconsciously, the mind scans for clues in the environment, which it uses to influence our purchasing actions.

So how do you do this? There are two particularly effective ways; through authority and scarcity. Authority is one of the most prominent triggers because we as people are predisposed to accept the viewpoints of authoritative people. That's why we are so willing to believe in the health advice we get from doctors, or the accuracy of street directions from a cop. And scarcity works well, because when we discover something will only be available for a short period of time, we act like fiends to get it. Not only this, but we add greater value on products that are scarce (like a Ferrari).

A simple way to exploit this tendency in marketing a product or service is to suggest that it's price will rise imminently. This is a sure way to generate interest.

"HABIT FORMING PRODUCTS ARE ONES THAT GRADUALLY FIND THEIR WAY INTO OUR LIVES. LIKE THE SMARTPHONE." - NIR EYAL

How can a company strive to make their product habit forming? By trying the Hook model.

This model is a cycle that consists of four steps and when repeated enough, will lead the user to form a habit around the product in question:

1) The Trigger: An external event that gets us to try a product for the first time. Like a TV commercial.
2) The Action: What we need to do in order to use the product. Like registering on an online community.
3) The Reward: The fulfillment of the need that originally motivated us to take action.
4) The Investment: Something of value that we have invested in the product, such as time, money or information.

The last step leads back to the start of the cycle and as these steps are repeated over and over again, the user starts to develop internal triggers instead of external ones. The user eventually becomes hooked and doesn't think if she wants the product, but rather just does it.

"PEOPLE WILL FORGET WHAT YOU SAY, BUT THEY MAY
NEVER FORGET HOW YOU MADE THEM FEEL."
- MAYA ANGELOU

Hollywood writers live by the rule that their words should stir up emotions in viewers. They know that when language touches a person's feelings, it leaves a lasting impression in their memory. The key to accomplishing this is to find words that either apply to a situation everyone is familiar with, or to their personal life experience. Martin Luther King Jr.'s "I have a dream" speech is a great example of applying to a situation. This speech not only applied to the black members of his audience, but to the guiding principles of all Americans.

Another excellent tool to use is to ask questions. Addressing your audience with a question begs a direct response that will trigger a thought process and lead them to a conclusion. So for example, when trying to curate the perfect Facebook ad, ask a question in your content. Lead your customers to the final destination because they were wanting to answer a question. Successful blogs do this all the time, just the other day I read a blog post via Facebook who's post title was 'Are you a passionate tech entrepreneur?'. My automatic response (especially as someone who is in digital) was 'Ooh! I must read this!'.

"DON'T CREATE A COMPANY CULTURE BUILT ON FEAR, THIS FEAR WILL LEAD TO INDIVIDUALS WHO ARE AFRAID OF CHANGE." - ROHIT BHARGAVA

Imagine you're on your way to the airport in an Uber. Your driver strikes up a conversation and because he turns out to be a great guy, you make note of his number, give him a rave review and promise to keep in touch with him the next time you might need a ride somewhere.

As you get to the airport and board your flight, the airline attendants present a friendly face, but everything they say seems to come directly from a handbook. In short, none of them show personality.

Whose praises will you sing to your friends and colleagues: the taxi driver or the flight attendants? Obviously the Uber driver.

Long gone are the times of 'corporate culture'. Today the success of one's company depends on creating a bond with your customer, although many companies still to this day still deny Facebook and remain disconnected - (don't get me started!).

"YOU ARE AT ANY GIVEN TIME, SURROUNDED BY SIMPLE, OBVIOUS SOLUTIONS THAT CAN DRAMATICALLY INCREASE YOUR SUCCESS." - JAY ABRAHAM

Imagine you are in the market for a dog and you find two dogs of equal breed, mix, shape and size (I'm not a dog expert here). One dog costs $750, and the other dog costs $1000. However, the seller of the more expensive dog offers you a 30 day back money guarantee to see if you and the dog like each other. They also offer you free training and free first set of shots, plus a puppy starter kit that includes a food and water pot (I'm just trying to be creative here). And if you do change your mind about the dog, they have also offered to come pick it up for free.

All of a sudden, the $250 difference doesn't seem so expensive anymore and buying the more expensive dog seems like the obvious choice.

So here's the deal, to win over the most amount of clients, you must offer the most bang for their buck. Because for every original business idea out there, there are 5 that follow right behind it (I tell you from experience). You must learn to stay ahead of the competition by always 1) offering more than they expect and 2) making the purchasing decision as easy and flawless as possible - think Amazon Prime.

"AWARENESS PRECEDES CHOICE, AND CHOICE PRECEDES RESULTS."- ROBIN SHARMA

Brand awareness leads to market outcome. And the more your brand is visible, the more you can elevate your creativity and in turn also allows you to gain trust which ultimately leads to more business.

So what are some of the top ways to quickly begin getting your brand noticed? Here are some sure fire ways you can get started to making your way out on top:

1) Design a website that's about YOU, your business should have a website of it's own. Your brand is NOT your business, you are your own brand.

2) Create a unique blog and write unique articles with catchy titles. Share these blogs on your social networks with a bit.ly link so you can track your analytics

3) Share your accolades and accomplishments on your 'About Me' page. Don't be shy! People need to know what makes you YOU.

4) Create an opt in offer that your readers can sign up for - NOT a newsletter! In turn you can create a badass email list of people who adore you and want to hear from you.

"NETWORKING IS MORE ABOUT "FARMING" THEN IT IS ABOUT "HUNTING". IT'S ABOUT CULTIVATING RELATIONSHIPS." – DR. IVAN MISNER.

Imagine that the average person knows approximately 200 people, and on average you could connect to just about anyone around the world within 3 levels of your network.

Just recently, I went back into my old business email database (Youzus) and downloaded the CSV file of past clients, would you imagine I had more than 10,000 people I had touched base with over the course of 3 years? That's people who will actually remember me in some way shape or form. Now, imagine what will happen when I actually email these past clients with new products I'm going to be giving away (such as this book!). Because they already know me, or have done business with me in the past, I'm familiar and trustworthy t them. I don't have to re-introduce myself or try to sell to new customers.

Try this with your current email. Download a CSV file of your existing email database and reach out to them. See what they have to say if you were to sell them a product or service. Remember, people like doing business with people they know and trust.

"DON'T LOOK FOR THE NEXT OPPORTUNITY, THE ONE YOU HAVE IN YOUR HAND IS THE OPPORTUNITY." - PAUL ARDEN

We are always looking for the perfect client and it almost never happens. Or you're probably working on a job, brief or proposal right now thinking let's just get this over and done with. Or "this client is a pain in the ass, I don't care to go above and beyond."

However, whatever you have right now, that's the one. You must make it the best experience for the client you can - period. It may not be the greatest piece of work you've ever done, but at least you can lay your head at night knowing you tried your best.

See, good proposals, clients, customers don't just come along. And you are lucky if they often do! But you must continue to do the best work, because it's often even in the worst of situations we face that we are taught lessons for when those amazing opportunities do come our way.

As Paul Arden said, "Successful solutions are often created by people rebelling against bad briefs (or clients).

AS WE LEARN TO SPEAK APPROPRIATELY, WE LOSE SOMETHING IN AUTHENTICITY." - SHERYL SANDBERG

There have been many times where I've written content for a Facebook or Instagram post - or - times where I originally wanted to say one thing and ended up saying another in an email that ended up being too carefully constructed and looked like I should have been wearing a nun's cap when I wrote it. The point being is that more often than not, we end up erasing and deleting things to make them more appropriate, or to not offend anyone. And what ends up happening is we take the authenticity out of the equation which in turn effects the whole brilliance behind the original piece and the entire thing loses its lacklustre.

Sometimes in marketing or when connecting with your clients, you have to go with the thing you wanted to say first because I can almost guarantee it's the 'thing' that will come across as the most realest and make the most amount of sense. Because if you truly think about it, how many people do you know that speak appropriate 100% of the time? I don't know about you, but most of the people I know in my circle respond the most when I throw down an F bomb or treat them like my best friend.

AS WE LEARN TO SPEAK APPROPRIATELY, WE LOSE "OF

ALL OF OUR INVENTIONS FOR MASS COMMUNICATION,
PICTURES STILL SPEAK THE MOST UNIVERSALLY
UNDERSTOOD LANGUAGE." - WALT DISNEY

I tell this to clients all the time. Your content is a very powerful form of communication. In one post you must evoke emotion, intimacy, and engagement, and the only way to do this is through visual storytelling.

Your message should be impactful and memorable and a video or picture can do both of these when quick stories are told quickly but thoughtfully. Who remembers all the Gerber baby commercials? And to think they have an Instagram account now too! Who doesn't love adorable giggling babies - right? In fact, according to KISSMetrics, content with relevant images gets 94% more views than content without relevant images.

So the next time you go to create a visual, whether it is a picture or a video, ensure it has one of the universally recognized expressions: joy, surprise, sadness, anger, disgust and fear. And most importantly, ensure it is authentic. People can read right through the fake stuff and they know when you are lying - bad for business and will come bite you in the butt. Remember, you want to build a memorable brand with a great reputation.

"YOUR WEBSITE IS YOUR GREATEST ASSET. MORE PEOPLE VIEW YOUR WEBPAGES THAN ANYTHING ELSE."
- AMANDA SIBLEY

Your website represents you, think of it as your business card. Since we live in a day and age where most interactions happen over the phone or online, your website must be the one place where people can come to learn about you and/or your business. Taking into consideration how quick people are to make a first impression, you must look at your website objectively and decide if it's time for a revamp. There have been countless times in the past where I haven't called someone through their website simply because of the way their website looked.

However, website design aside for a second, you must also add content to make it convincing. Don't forget to add blogs with catchy titles that are informative and to the point. This will show your visitors that you a) know what you are talking about and b) are a to the point business person that takes their position seriously.

Another note to point out is to ensure your navigation is easy to use and your site isn't overflowing with information. Remember, we live a 30 second world of tweets, no one has time to read a novel of a website.

"DON'T BE BORING...THINK ABOUT YOUR FIRST BRAND IMPRESSION: HOW CAN YOU MAKE IT AWESOMER?" - SCOTT EDWARDS

Scott actually shared a great example of how a bank called Simple Bank, an online banking company and software, earned trust with their customers by making some minor tweaks to a notoriously boring task associated with banking: picking your PIN. One way Simple Bank did this was by changing the PIN selection interface on their website.

When a customer chose a PIN on Simple bank's website, the bank gave some feedback in return. So for example, if they entered a pin on the site as '1234', a common and non-secure pin choice, instead of just rejecting the pin, the Simple bank populated text underneath that read: "This PIN is ridiculous". This showed the customers that the bank had a personality, and the entire site was actually built with this functionality in mind.

We can even take 'out of office' emails as an example. The next time you plan on heading out of town and turn on this notification, why not try to be a bit clever? You could write something like, "Sorry my 'out of office' gave you false hope of my enthusiastic and swift response...";)

"HIGHLIGHT THE PRODUCT BY MAKING IT THE HERO."
- DAVID OGILVY

What's the difference between selling Soap A and selling Soap B, if both soaps have basically the same properties and are essentially the same product? Providing something the other doesn't. Basically, making your product the hero and the star.

As we saw in the case of Dove, they participate in social networks, encouraging debates to define what real beauty is in response to low female self-esteem caused by society and the media. If there are lots of similar products out there, yours has got to provide the same or more than the others and bring something extra to the table. Individuals must identify with the values of the brand and everything the product represents. Ogilvy says: "there are no dull products, only dull writers."

Another huge brand that managed to position itself in the minds of consumers is Apple. Apple knows how to whisper their beliefs in the ears of their audience. There are tons of MP3 players and Tablets on the market, but an iPod or an iPad gives you so much more than just hours of music and videos. Apple's positioning strategy focuses primarily on emotions and the consumer's lifestyle, their imagination, passion, dreams, hopes, aspirations, and they promise to make people's lives easier.

"NO MATTER THE TALENT OR THE EFFORTS, THERE ARE THINGS THAT COME WITH TIME. YOU CAN'T CREATE A BABY IN A MONTH BY GETTING 9 WOMEN PREGNANT"
- WARREN BUFFETT

We all love immediacy, being able to have all the results here and now without having to wait for things come as soon as possible. But in marketing things don't function this way and there are actions no matter how fast we implement them, they need time to produce results.

Learn to respect time and think that wanting to speed up the results can lead to making errors that could have been avoided and that they can stagger your digital marketing strategy.

This is something that happened to Apple when they decided to eliminate Google Maps from the devices in favor of their own map application, they rushed into wanting to offer their own service when it wasn't 100% presentable and the case ended in the dismissal of an executive and the public apology from the president of the technology giant. You don't want this to be you. I personally had to endure something like this in my own career, and trust me when I say I wish I had waited instead of jumping the gun.

When creating your product, don't worry about the competition or how fast you need to put something out. All timing is divine and you must trust your gut!

Now Go And Build A Bad Ass Brand!

www.ingramcontent.com/pod-product-compliance
Lightning Source LLC
Chambersburg PA
CBHW080222220526
45468CB00018B/2937